FIFA WORLD CUP QUIZ

300 QUESTIONS ON PLAYERS, TEAMS, TROPHIES
& LOTS MORE TO TEST YOUR KNOWLEDGE

By
QuizGuy

FIFA WORLD CUP QUIZ: 300 Questions on Players, Teams, Trophies & Lots More to Test Your Knowledge © 2020 by QuizGuy. All Rights Reserved. No part of this publication may be reproduced or transmitted in any form or by any means, electronic, mechanical, including photocopying, recording, or any other information or storage and retrieval system, without the permission of the publisher.

Also, in the series...

Preface

"For a player or coach, there is nothing better than the World Cup."

Didier Deschamps

"There's nothing quite like a World Cup."

Michael Owen

"Winning the World Cup was a dream come true."

Miroslav Klose

"It is the dream of all the children of the world to play in the World Cup final."

Roberto Baggio

The FIFA World Cup started in 1930 and this competition gives the opportunity for national association football teams to compete on an international stage. The FIFA World Cup takes place every four years and it is one of most fantastic competitions on the sporting calendar. The competition has provided countless memories and plenty of nail-biting moments. The FIFA World Cup is the pinnacle of international football and this global competition is watched by billions of people across the world.

The FIFA World Cup Quiz is fun and informative and will provide hours of entertainment for all of those who love this competition.

Hopefully, the quiz will remind you of some of the incredible talents that have graced this fantastic competition over the years.

QuizGuy has designed a quiz to test your knowledge on the FIFA World Cup. This quiz consists of 20 rounds each made up of 15 questions. You will be tested on lots of different topics related to players, teams, trophies, and lots more.

Now is the time to put your knowledge to the test! Good Luck!

Table of Contents

Round 1: All Time Team Records 1
    Round 1 Answers 3
Round 2: Player Records 4
    Round 2 Answers 6
Round 3: Final Records 7
    Round 3 Answers 9
Round 4: Locations 10
    Round 4 Answers 12
Round 5: Goalkeepers 13
    Round 5 Answers 15
Round 6 : Defenders 16
    Round 6 Answers 18
Round 7 : Midfielders 19
    Round 7 Answers 21
Round 8: Forwards 22
    Round 8 Answers 24
Round 9: Captains 25
    Round 9 Answers 27
Round 10: Managers 28
    Round 10 Answers 30
Round 11: Host Nations 31
    Round 11 Answers 33
Round 12: Amazing Goals 34
    Round 12 Answers 36

Round 13: Memorable Moments 37
    Round 13 Answers 39
Round 14: Player Appearances and Goal Records 40
    Round 14 Answers 42
Round 15: Hat-tricks, 4 goals & 5 goals 43
    Round 15 Answers 45
Round 16: Defenders 2nd Round 46
    Round 16 Answers 48
Round 17: Midfielders 2nd Round.. 49
    Round 17 Answers 51
Round 18: Forwards 2nd Round 52
    Round 18 Answers 54
Round 19: Penalty Shootout Trivia 55
    Round 19 Answers 57
Round 20: Challenging Trivia 58
    Round 20 Answers 60
Congratulations! 61

Round 1: All Time Team Records

1. Which team are the current World Cup champions after winning the tournament in 2018?

2. Can you name the team that has won the World Cup the most times?

3. Which nation has finished as runners-up the most times in the history of the competition?

4. Which team won the first ever World Cup in 1930?

5. England have won the competition on one occasion. Which year did they win the World Cup?

6. Which two nations have won the World Cup exactly four times?

7. Can you name the team that has lost the most finals without ever winning the competition?

8. When did Italy last win a World Cup?

9. How many times have France won the competition?

10. Which two European teams have a 100% record in World Cup finals?

11. When was the last time a South American team won the World Cup?

12. How many times have Uruguay won the World Cup?

13. Can you name the first European team that won a World Cup?

14. How many times have Argentina won the competition?

15. Which two Europeans teams have appeared in just one final but have never won the competition?

Round 1 Answers

1. France
2. Brazil
3. Germany
4. Uruguay
5. 1966
6. Italy and Germany
7. Netherlands
8. 2006
9. Two times
10. England and Spain
11. 2002
12. Two times
13. Italy
14. Two times
15. Sweden and Croatia

Round 2: Player Records

16. One player holds a record for winning the World Cup the most times. He won the competition on three different occasions. Who is the player?

17. Which player has scored the most goals at World Cups?

18. One Mexican player holds a record for captaining his nation at five different World Cups. Can you name the player?

19. Can you name the player that holds the record for winning the most matches at World Cups? The player in question, was on the winning team on 17 different occasions.

20. Which player holds the record for the most appearances at World Cups? He is German and has made a total of 25 appearances.

21. Can you name the Turkish player that has scored the quickest ever goal in World Cup history? He scored after 11 seconds.

22. Can you name the two players that have scored at least one goal in a record 11 matches?

23. Who is the oldest player to score a goal at a World Cup? He did this at 42 years and 39 days.

24. Who is the youngest ever player to score at a World Cup? He did this at 17 years and 239 days.

25. Can you name the player that scored the fastest ever brace in World Cup history? He did this in a 2014 World Cup semi-final.

26. Which player has received a record seven yellow cards in the competition? The player in question, comes from Argentina.

27. Can you name the only player to score a hat-trick in a World Cup final?

28. Two goalkeepers hold the record for keeping the most clean sheets in the competition. They both kept a total of 10 clean sheets. One is from England and the other is from France. Can you name them?

29. Two players hold the record for receiving the most red cards. They were both sent off twice. One player is from France and the other is from Cameroon. Can you name the two players?

30. One Brazilian player holds the record for coming on as a substitute the most amount of times at World Cups. He made 11 appearances as a substitute. Can you name him?

Round 2 Answers

16. Pele
17. Miroslav Klose
18. Rafael Marquez
19. Miroslav Klose
20. Lothar Matthaus
21. Hakan Sukur
22. Ronaldo and Miroslav Klose
23. Roger Milla
24. Pele
25. Toni Kroos
26. Javier Mascherano
27. Geoff Hurst
28. Peter Shilton and Fabien Barthez
29. Zinedine Zidane and Rigobert Song
30. Denilson

Round 3: Final Records

31. Who is the only player to score an own goal in a World Cup final? The player in question is from Croatia.

32. Can you name the youngest ever player to make an appearance in a World Cup final? He did this at 17 years and 249 days.

33. Which player was the first substitute to score the winning goal in a World Cup final?

34. Who scored the latest ever goal in a World Cup final? It was scored in the 120th minute of the game.

35. Which nation has been in the World Cup final a record eight times?

36. Can you name the first captain to be sent off in a World Cup final?

37. Only one nation has had two players sent off in the same game which is a World Cup final. Can you name the team?

38. The record for the most amount of goals by one team in a World Cup final, stands at five goals. Which team achieved this?

39. Which nation scored the quickest ever goal in a World Cup final? The goal was scored after 90 seconds.

40. Can you name the only two teenagers to score in a World Cup final?

41. Two teams have played each other a record three times in World Cup finals. Can you name the two teams?

42. Which two nations played out the only 0-0 in a World Cup final?

43. Can you name the player that holds the record for appearing in three different World Cup finals? He won two of these finals and lost one.

44. Can you name the team that has received the most bookings in one World Cup final? The team in question received a total of nine bookings.

45. Who is the oldest player to make an appearance in a World Cup final?

Round 3 Answers

31. Mario Mandzukic
32. Pele
33. Mario Gotze
34. Geoff Hurst
35. Germany
36. Zinedine Zidane
37. Argentina
38. Brazil
39. Netherlands
40. Pele and Kylian Mbappe
41. Argentina and Germany
42. Brazil and Italy
43. Cafu
44. Netherlands
45. Dino Zoff

Round 4: Locations

46. Which country will host their first World Cup in 2022?

47. Only one World Cup to date, has been hosted by two countries. Can you name the two countries that hosted the competition together?

48. Which country hosted the first World Cup to be held in Africa?

49. Can you name the country that hosted the first ever World Cup in 1930?

50. One World Cup was hosted by the United States of America. Which year did they host the competition?

51. Can you name the two countries that were losing finalists when hosting the competition?

52. Only one country that has hosted the World Cup two times, has had over 100,000 people in attendance for both finals. Can you name the country?

53. When did France last host the World Cup?

54. Can you name the first European country to host a World Cup?

55. Which stadium holds the record for the largest attendance for a World Cup final?

56. Spain hosted the World Cup in 1982, which stadium was the final played at?

57. When was the last time that Argentina hosted a World Cup?

58. Which country hosted their first World Cup in 2018?

59. Can you name the six countries that have won the World Cup when hosting the competition?

60. Can you name the five countries that have hosted the World Cup two times?

Round 4 Answers

46. Qatar
47. Japan and South Korea
48. South Africa
49. Uruguay
50. 1994
51. Brazil and Sweden
52. Mexico
53. 1998
54. Italy
55. Maracana, Rio de Janeiro, Brazil
56. Santiago Bernabeu
57. 1978
58. Russia
59. Uruguay, Italy, England, Germany, Argentina and France
60. Mexico, Italy, France, Germany and Brazil

Round 5: Goalkeepers

61. Which goalkeeper played in the final in 1994 and 1998 for Brazil?

62. Who was England's goalkeeper for the 1966 final?

63. Jan Jongbloed made appearances in consecutive finals for which team?

64. Who played in goal for Italy in the 1994 World Cup final?

65. Can you name the French goalkeeper that played in the final in 1998 and 2006?

66. Which country did Sepp Maier win a World Cup with?

67. Who was in goal for Brazil when they conceded 7 goals to Germany in World Cup 2014?

68. Can you name the goalkeeper that started the 2014 World Cup final for Germany?

69. Which goalkeeper started for Italy in the 2006 final?

70. Can you name Croatia's goalkeeper for the 2018 final?

71. Which Brazilian goalkeeper started in the 2002 final?

72. Can you name Argentina's goalkeeper for the 2014 World Cup final?

73. Which goalkeeper started the 2010 final for the Netherlands?

74. Who is the youngest ever goalkeeper to save a penalty in a shootout? He did this at 21 years and 27 days at the 2002 World Cup.

75. Who is the oldest goalkeeper to save a penalty in a shootout? He did this at 36 years and 232 days at the 2006 World Cup.

Round 5 Answers

61. Claudio Taffarel
62. Gordon Banks
63. Netherlands
64. Gianluca Pagliuca
65. Fabien Barthez
66. Germany
67. Julio Cesar
68. Manuel Neuer
69. Gianluigi Buffon
70. Danijel Subasic
71. Marcos
72. Sergio Romero
73. Maarten Stekelenburg
74. Iker Casillas
75. Jens Lehmann

Round 6 : Defenders

76. Which defender received the Silver Ball Award for his outstanding performances at the 2006 World Cup?

77. Which two Barcelona defenders played as centre backs for Spain in the 2010 World Cup final?

78. Which Brazilian full backs started in the final of both the 1998 and 2002 World Cups?

79. Can you name the French defender that was sent off in the 1998 World Cup final?

80. Can you name the German defender that captained his side to victory in the 2014 World Cup final?

81. Which Italian defender is the leading appearance maker for his country at World Cups?

82. Who was Spain's captain for the 2018 World Cup?

83. Which Argentinian left back captained his side at the 2006 World Cup?

84. Which Brazilian centre back started in the final of both the 1994 and 1998 World Cups?

85. Can you name Germany's centre back pairing for their 2014 World Cup final success?

86. Which England defender had a headed goal disallowed in the round of 16 tie against Argentina at the 1998 World Cup?

87. Which Uruguayan defender was the captain for his side at the 2018 World Cup?

88. Who was captain for Germany when they won the 1974 World Cup?

89. Who captained Italy in the 1994 World Cup final?

90. Can you name the Italian player that scored in the 2006 World Cup final?

Round 6 Answers

76. Fabio Cannavaro
77. Carlos Puyol and Gerard Pique
78. Cafu and Roberto Carlos
79. Marcel Desailly
80. Philipp Lahm
81. Paolo Maldini
82. Sergio Ramos
83. Juan Pablo Sorin
84. Aldair
85. Mats Hummels and Jerome Boateng
86. Sol Campbell
87. Diego Godin
88. Franz Beckenbauer
89. Franco Baresi
90. Marco Materazzi

Round 7 : Midfielders

91. Can you name the Colombian midfielder that finished the 2014 World Cup as top goal scorer?

92. Which Croatian midfielder captained his side to the World Cup final in 2018?

93. Who received the player of the tournament award for England when they won the 1966 World Cup?

94. Can you name the French midfielder that scored in the 2018 World Cup final?

95. Which Brazilian winger won player of the tournament at the 1962 World Cup?

96. Which midfielder won player of the tournament at the 2018 World Cup?

97. Which German midfielder scored three goals at the 2002 World Cup? These goals helped his side reach the final of the tournament.

98. Which midfielder won player of the tournament at the 2006 World Cup?

99. Who was the Spanish player that scored the only goal of the 2010 World Cup final?

100. Which Atletico Madrid midfielder was joint second goal scorer with three goals at the 2006 World Cup? The player in question, is from Argentina.

101. Can you name the midfielder that captained England at the 2010 World Cup?

102. Which midfielder is Australia's all-time top goal scorer in World Cup history with five goals?

103. Can you name the Netherlands' midfielder that scored a penalty in the 1974 World Cup final?

104. Which England midfielder scored in the 1966 World Cup final?

105. Zinedine Zidane scored two of France's three goals in the 1998 final. Who scored the other goal for France?

Round 7 Answers

91. James Rodriguez
92. Luka Modric
93. Bobby Charlton
94. Paul Pogba
95. Garrincha
96. Luka Modric
97. Michael Ballack
98. Zinedine Zidane
99. Andres Iniesta
100. Maxi Rodriguez
101. Steven Gerrard
102. Tim Cahill
103. Johan Neeskens
104. Martin Peters
105. Emmanuel Petit

Round 8: Forwards

106. Can you name the English player that won the Golden Boot Award at the 1986 World Cup?

107. Which player finished the 2002 World Cup as top goal scorer with eight goals?

108. Which forward is Argentina's all-time top scorer in World Cup history with 10 goals?

109. Can you name the Bulgarian international that finished as joint top goal scorer at the 1994 World Cup? He scored six goals in the competition.

110. Which Brazilian player scored a brace in the 2002 World Cup final?

111. Who finished as top goal scorer at the 2006 World Cup?

112. Can you name Denmark's all-time top goal scorer in World Cup history? He has scored five goals in the competition.

113. Can you name Spain's all-time top goal scorer in World Cup history? He has scored a total of nine goals in the competition.

114. Which Brazilian striker started the final in both the 1994 and 1998 World Cups?

115. Can you name the Italian player that finished the 1982 World Cup as the top goal scorer of the competition? He scored six goals at that World Cup.

116. Which two Brazilian forwards both scored a brace in the 1958 World Cup final?

117. Who is the only Portuguese player to have won the Golden Boot Award?

118. Which two players started as Italy's forwards in their 2006 World Cup final victory?

119. Can you name the Croatian international that won the Golden Boot Award at the 1998 World Cup?

120. At the 1970 World Cup, a German player finished the competition as top goal scorer. Can you name him?

Round 8 Answers

106. Gary Lineker
107. Ronaldo
108. Gabriel Batistuta
109. Hristo Stoichkov
110. Ronaldo
111. Miroslav Klose
112. Jon Dahl Tomasson
113. David Villa
114. Bebeto
115. Paolo Rossi
116. Pele and Vava
117. Eusebio
118. Francesco Totti and Luca Toni
119. Davor Suker
120. Gerd Muller

Round 9: Captains

121. Can you name the player that captained his Argentina side to the 2014 World Cup final?

122. Which goalkeeper captained his side in the 2018 World Cup final?

123. Who was England's captain when they won the competition in 1966?

124. Which Italy player was captain when they won the World Cup in 2006?

125. Can you name the goalkeeper that captained Spain to World Cup glory in 2010?

126. During the 2002 World Cup, the Republic of Ireland captain was sent home after a disagreement with the manager. Who was this captain?

127. Can you name the Netherlands' captain when they were losing finalists in 1974?

128. Which player led his nation to World Cup glory as captain in 1986?

129. Who was Germany's captain for the 2002 World Cup final?

130. Which England captain was top goal scorer at the 2018 World Cup?

131. Which Brazilian captain led his side to victory in the 1970 World Cup final? He also scored in the game.

132. Can you name the Brazil captain, when they won the 2002 World Cup final?

133. Can you name the German player that suffered two World Cup final defeats as captain?

134. Which played led his Hungarian side out as captain in the 1954 World Cup final? He also scored in the game.

135. Can you name the player that captained Brazil in the final of the 1994 and 1998 World Cups?

Round 9 Answers

121. Lionel Messi
122. Hugo Lloris
123. Bobby Moore
124. Fabio Cannavaro
125. Iker Casillas
126. Roy Keane
127. Johan Cruyff
128. Diego Maradona
129. Oliver Kahn
130. Harry Kane
131. Carlos Alberto
132. Cafu
133. Karl-Heinz Rummenigge
134. Ferenc Puskas
135. Dunga

Round 10: Managers

136. Who was the manager of France when they exited the competition at the group stage in 2010? Behind the scenes they had lots of problems at this World Cup and the players refused to train at one stage.

137. Which manager famously sent Roy Keane home from World Cup 2002?

138. Can you name the manager that led Brazil to World Cup glory in 2002?

139. Who was the manager of Germany for their 2014 World Cup win?

140. Can you name the foreign manager that led England to two quarter finals in 2002 and 2006?

141. Which manager took Germany to the final of the 2002 World Cup?

142. Who was England's manager for their 1966 World Cup win?

143. Which manager led Italy to glory at the 2006 World Cup?

144. Who was manager of England at the 1998 World Cup?

145. Can you name the manager that took South Korea to the semi-finals of the 2002 World Cup?

146. Which two managers have been knocked out of the World Cup at the semi-final stage with England?

147. Who was Germany's manager when they were defeated in the 1986 World Cup final?

148. Can you name the manager that oversaw Spain at the 2010 World Cup, where they were crowned as winners of the tournament for the first time?

149. One manager holds two records. One record is managing at six World Cups and the other is managing five different teams at World Cups. Can you name him?

150. Which manager led France to World Cup glory in 1998?

Round 10 Answers

136. Raymond Domenech
137. Mick McCarthy
138. Luiz Felipe Scolari
139. Joachim Low
140. Sven-Goran Eriksson
141. Rudi Voller
142. Sir Alf Ramsey
143. Marcello Lippi
144. Glenn Hoddle
145. Guus Hiddink
146. Sir Bobby Robson and Gareth Southgate
147. Franz Beckenbauer
148. Vincente del Bosque
149. Carlos Alberto Parreira
150. Aime Jacquet

Round 11: Host Nations

151. Who was the manager of Germany when they hosted the competition in 2006?

152. Which country knocked the United States of America out of the competition when they were the hosts? This was in a round of 16 game at the 1994 World Cup.

153. Who was Russia's captain when they hosted the competition in 2018?

154. Which team knocked out Germany when they hosted the competition in 2006?

155. South Africa only won one game when they hosted the competition in 2010. They exited the World Cup at the group stage. Which team did they win against?

156. Which team defeated hosts Chile in the semi-finals of the 1962 World Cup?

157. Which team beat Brazil in the 1950 World Cup final? Brazil hosted this competition.

158. Who knocked Russia out of the 2018 World Cup? Russia lost at the quarter-final stage on penalties.

159. Which team knocked out hosts Mexico in the 1986 World Cup? Mexico lost on penalties in this quarter final game.

160. The hosts Switzerland were defeated 7-5 at the quarter final stage of the 1954 World Cup. Can you name the team that knocked Switzerland out of the competition?

161. Which team knocked Italy out at the semi-final stage of the 1990 World Cup?

162. Mexico were knocked out at the quarter finals stage when they hosted the 1970 World Cup. Which team knocked them out of the competition?

163. Which team knocked out the hosts France in a 1938 World Cup quarter final?

164. Can you name Germany's captain when they hosted the World Cup in 2006?

165. Which nation knocked out joint hosts Japan in the 2002 World Cup? This was in a second-round game.

Round 11 Answers

151. Jurgen Klinsmann
152. Brazil
153. Igor Akinfeev
154. Italy
155. France
156. Brazil
157. Uruguay
158. Croatia
159. Germany
160. Austria
161. Argentina
162. Italy
163. Italy
164. Michael Ballack
165. Turkey

Round 12: Amazing Goals

166. Which Colombian player scored an outstanding volley against Uruguay in a second-round game at the 2014 World Cup? He chested the ball swiveled and volleyed the ball off the bar and into the back of the net.

167. Can you name the Italian player that scored one of the goals of the 1990 World Cup against the then named Czechoslovakia? The Italian player beat several players and then did a feint past the last defender before beating the goalkeeper.

168. Can you name the Germany player that scored a great 30-yard strike against Costa Rica in the 2006 World Cup? He made it 4-2 to Germany with this tremendous strike after receiving a pass from a free kick.

169. Which Romanian player scored a memorable goal against Colombia in World Cup 1994? He looped the ball over the goalkeeper from 40 yards out catching the goalkeeper out of position.

170. Which Netherlands player scored one of the goals of the 1998 World Cup in a game against Argentina? The player in question collected a 60-yard pass from Frank de Boer, touched it through a defender's legs and then volleyed into the goal with the outside of his right foot.

171. During a game between Argentina and England in a quarter final match, one England player scored a terrific individual goal. This was at the 1998 World Cup. This player collected the ball by the halfway line and beat several Argentina players before unleashing a right footed effort into the back of the net. Can you name the player that scored this goal?

172. Can you name the Netherlands player that opened the scoring against Uruguay in one of the 2010 World Cup semi-finals? He received the ball a long way out and unleashed a powerful left footed strike which flew into to the top corner of the goal.

173. Which England player scored an amazing volley which took his team through to the quarter finals of the 1990 World Cup? This goal was scored in extra time against Belgium.

174. During a stunning 5-1 victory for the Netherlands over Spain, one player scored a beautiful leaping header. This was in the group stage of the 2014 World Cup. Can you name the player that scored this goal?

175. Which player scored the 'Goal of the Century' during the 1986 World Cup against England? For the goal, he dribbled past five England players, took the ball past the goalkeeper, and slotted the ball into the net with his left foot.

176. During the 2014 World Cup group stage, Australia played against the Netherlands. In the game, an Australian player scored a sensational left footed volley from inside the penalty area. Which player scored this goal?

177. Can you name the Argentinian player that scored one of the goals of the 2006 World Cup? He chested a long pass from Juan Pablo Sorin before volleying the ball into the top corner with his left foot. This was in a second-round tie against Mexico.

178. During the 2006 World Cup, Argentina beat Serbia and Montenegro 6-0. The second goal was a fantastic team goal that consisted of 24 passes. Can you name the player that scored the goal?

179. Which Brazilian player scored after a fantastic team move in the 1970 World Cup final? He received a pass from Pele before firing into the goal making it 4-1 to Brazil. This goal was widely considered one of the greatest goals in World Cup history.

180. Can you name the Scotland player that scored a fantastic goal against the Netherlands at the 1978 World Cup? The player in question played a one-two with Dalglish before running into the area and scoring past the goalkeeper.

Round 12 Answers

166. James Rodriguez
167. Roberto Baggio
168. Torsten Frings
169. Gheorghe Hagi
170. Dennis Bergkamp
171. Michael Owen
172. Giovanni van Bronckhorst
173. David Platt
174. Robin van Persie
175. Diego Maradona
176. Tim Cahill
177. Maxi Rodriguez
178. Esteban Cambiasso
179. Carlos Alberto
180. Archie Gemmill

Round 13: Memorable Moments

181. Which England player famously did a 'salmon dive' towards the ball in his own penalty area to attempt to stop his team conceding a goal at the 2010 World Cup? This was in a game against Slovenia.

182. Brazilian player Rivaldo was involved in a controversial moment at the 2002 World Cup. A player on the opposing team kicked the ball at his thigh but Rivaldo pretended the ball hit him in the face and got the player sent off. Which team were Brazil playing in this game?

183. Which player helped Argentina knock England out of a quarter final at the 1986 World Cup, by scoring a controversial goal with his hand?

184. Wayne Rooney was sent off for a stamp on a Portugal player in a 2006 World Cup quarter final. After Rooney was sent off, one Portuguese player was caught on camera winking. The same player protested to the referee that Rooney should be sent off. Who was the Portugal player?

185. During a 2010 World Cup quarter final game between Uruguay and Ghana, one Uruguayan player was sent off for a blatant handball on the goal line. Can you name the player? Ghana missed the penalty that they were given and later lost the penalty shootout.

186. Zinedine Zidane was sent off for a headbutt during the 2006 World Cup final. Which Italian player did he headbutt?

187. David Beckham was sent off during a quarter final at World Cup 1998 for kicking out at a player. Which player did Beckham kick out at?

188. Which Netherlands defender was sent off in a game after fouling and spitting at Rudi Voller? Rudi Voller was also sent off in the same incident. This was at World Cup 1990.

189. Defending champions France went out at the group stage of the 2002 World Cup. They lost their opening game 1-0 to a team from Africa. Which team did they lose against?

190. Which Netherlands player had a turn named after him after pulling off a sensational piece of skill in a World Cup game against Sweden in 1974?

191. Can you name the England player that was in tears after picking up a yellow card during one of the 1990 World Cup semi-finals? The yellow card meant he would be suspended for the final if his team reached that stage.

192. In the group stages of the 1970 World Cup, Pele did a downward header with resulted in an outstanding save from a goalkeeper. This was often referred to as the 'Save of the Century.' Which goalkeeper made the save?

193. Which player emerged as one of the main stars of World Cup 1990? This player did a dance by the corner flag after scoring each goal. The player in question scored four goals at the tournament.

194. Graham Poll refereed a match between Croatia and Australia at the 2006 World Cup. The referee issued three yellow cards to one player before sending him off. Which player did Poll show three yellow cards to during the game?

195. Luis Suarez was banned from football for a period of four months after biting an Italian player during a game at the 2014 World Cup. Which player did Suarez bite?

Round 13 Answers

181. John Terry
182. Turkey
183. Diego Maradona
184. Cristiano Ronaldo
185. Luis Suarez
186. Marco Materazzi
187. Diego Simeone
188. Frank Rijkaard
189. Senegal
190. Johan Cruyff
191. Paul Gascoigne
192. Gordon Banks
193. Roger Milla
194. Josip Simunic
195. Georgio Chiellini

Round 14: Player Appearances and Goal Records

196. Can you name the player that has made the most appearances at World Cups for Argentina?

197. Who is Brazil's leading appearance maker at World Cups? The player in question has made a total of 21 appearances for his country in the competition.

198. Which two players hold the record for the most appearances for France at World Cups?

199. Can you name the player that has made the most appearances at World Cups for Portugal?

200. Which player holds the records for the most appearances and the most goals scored at World Cups for Ghana?

201. Can you name the player that has made the most appearances at World Cups for Ivory Coast?

202. Who is Cameroon's leading goal scorer at World Cups? He has scored a total of five goals in the competition.

203. Which two players hold the record for the most appearances for Switzerland at World Cups? They both have played in 10 games.

204. Can you name the Republic of Ireland player that has played in the most games at World Cups for his country? He is a defender and played in a total of 13 games in the competition.

205. Which player holds the records for the most appearances and the most goals scored at World Cups for U.S.A.?

206. Which two players hold the record for the most appearances for Spain at World Cups? They both have played in 17 games.

207. Who is Sweden's leading appearance maker at World Cups? He has played in 13 games for his country in the competition.

208. Can you name Nigeria's record appearance maker in World Cups? He is a defender and he has played in a total of 10 games in the competition.

209. The record for the most appearances at a World Cup for an England player stands at 17. Can you name the player that holds this record?

210. Can you name the two players from the Netherlands that have made the most appearances for their country at World Cups? Both players have been involved in 17 games in the competition.

Round 14 Answers

196. Diego Maradona
197. Cafu
198. Fabien Barthez and Thierry Henry
199. Cristiano Ronaldo
200. Asamoah Gyan
201. Yaya Toure
202. Roger Milla
203. Stephan Lichtsteiner and Valon Behrami
204. Steve Staunton
205. Landon Donovan
206. Iker Casillas and Sergio Ramos
207. Henrik Larsson
208. Joseph Yobo
209. Peter Shilton
210. Robin Van Persie and Wesley Sneijder

Round 15: Hat-tricks, 4 goals & 5 goals

211. Can you name the Portuguese player that scored four goals against North Korea in a 5-3 victory for his team?

212. Which three England players have scored a hat-trick in a World Cup game?

213. An Argentinian player scored a hat-trick against Jamaica at the 1998 World Cup. Who was the player?

214. Can you name the Portuguese player that scored a hat-trick at the 2002 World Cup?

215. Who is the youngest player to score a hat-trick? He did this at 17 years and 244 days.

216. Can you name the German player that scored a hat-trick at the 2014 World Cup?

217. One Argentinian player scored a hat-trick against South Korea at the 2010 World Cup. Can you name him?

218. One team had two players score a hat-trick in an 8-0 victory over Cuba at the 1938 World Cup. Which team did these two hat-trick scorers play for?

219. Only one German player has scored more than one hat-trick at World Cups. Can you name him?

220. Which team did an England player score a hat-trick against at the 2018 World Cup?

221. Which team holds the record for the most hat-tricks scored at World Cups?

222. Which player scored a hat-trick for Switzerland at the 2014 World Cup? Switzerland beat Honduras 3-0 in this game.

223. Can you name the only player to score five goals in a World Cup game? He is from Russia and did this at World Cup 1994.

224. Who is the only French player to score more than one hat-trick at World Cups?

225. Can you name the oldest player to score a hat-trick at a World Cup? He did this at 33 years and 130 days. This was against Spain at the 2018 World Cup.

Round 15 Answers

211. Eusebio
212. Geoff Hurst, Gary Lineker and Harry Kane
213. Gabriel Batistuta
214. Pauleta
215. Pele
216. Thomas Muller
217. Gonzalo Higuain
218. Sweden
219. Gerd Muller
220. Panama
221. Germany
222. Xherdan Shaqiri
223. Oleg Salenko
224. Just Fontaine
225. Cristiano Ronaldo

Round 16: Defenders 2nd Round

226. Can you name the Brazilian centre back that started alongside Aldair in the 1998 World Cup final?

227. Which Republic of Ireland player captained his team at the 1990 World Cup?

228. Which Italian defender started alongside Franco Baresi as a centre back in the 1994 World Cup final?

229. Can you name the defender that scored both goals for France in a 2-1 semi-final victory over Croatia at the 1998 World Cup?

230. Can you name the two centre backs that both scored for Brazil in a 2-1 quarter final victory over Colombia at the 2014 World Cup?

231. Which defender scored the tournament winning last penalty for Italy in the 2006 final?

232. Which Germany player received the Silver Ball Award for his performances at the 1974 World Cup?

233. Which French centre back was suspended for the 1998 World Cup final after been red carded in the semi-final?

234. Who was the only German player to be sent off at World Cup 2018?

235. Can you name the Spanish centre back that scored the only goal of the game in a 1-0 victory over Germany? This was in the semi-final of the 2010 World Cup and took his team to the final.

236. Which two centre backs started the World Cup 2018 final for France?

237. Can you name the Croatian defender who is second on the all-time appearances list for his country at World Cups? He made

11 appearances for his country which is one behind Luka Modric who is the record holder with 12 appearances.

238. Which England player received the Silver Ball Award for his performances at the 1966 World Cup?

239. Which player started alongside Marcel Desailly as centre back for France in the 1998 World Cup final?

240. Can you name Argentina's two starting centre backs in the 2014 World Cup final?

Round 16 Answers

226. Junior Baiano
227. Mick McCarthy
228. Paolo Maldini
229. Lilian Thuram
230. David Luiz and Thiago Silva
231. Fabio Grosso
232. Franz Beckenbauer
233. Laurent Blanc
234. Jerome Boateng
235. Carlos Puyol
236. Raphael Varane and Samuel Umtiti
237. Dario Simic
238. Bobby Moore
239. Frank Leboeuf
240. Ezequiel Garay and Martin Demichelis

Round 17: Midfielders 2nd Round

241. Which Brazilian player scored the only goal for Brazil in their 7-1 defeat to Germany? This was at the semi-final stage of the 2014 World Cup.

242. Can you name the English player that scored the penalty in the 1-0 England victory over Argentina at World Cup 2002?

243. Which Italian midfielder received the Bronze Ball Award for his performances at the 2006 World Cup?

244. Can you name the Croatian midfielder that scored in the 2018 World Cup final?

245. Which two central midfielders started for Brazil in the World Cup final in 2002? Both players later earned a move to the Premier League.

246. Can you name the England midfielder that had a shot that crossed the goal line but was never given as a goal? This was at World Cup 2010 in a game against Germany in the second round.

247. Which two attacking midfielders have both scored five World Cup goals for France?

248. Which Brazilian player famously scored a free kick that looped over England's David Seaman at World Cup 2002?

249. Who was the only midfielder to start for Spain in the 2010 World Cup final that was not a Barcelona player?

250. Who is Senegal's leading goal scorer at World Cups? He scored a total of three goals in the competition and these were all at World Cup 2002.

251. Which Brazilian midfielder was wrongly sent off against Ivory Coast at World Cup 2010? After a player from the opposing team pretended, he had been elbowed.

252. Which Russian player scored four goals for the host nation at the 2018 World Cup?

253. Can you name the Netherlands midfielder that received the Silver Ball Award for his performances at the 2010 World Cup?

254. Which Spanish midfielder scored the winning penalty in the shootout against the Republic of Ireland at World Cup 2002? This was in a second-round game.

255. David Beckham scored his three World Cup goals against three different South American teams. Can you name the teams he scored against?

Round 17 Answers

241. Oscar
242. David Beckham
243. Andrea Pirlo
244. Ivan Perisic
245. Giberto Silva and Kleberson
246. Frank Lampard
247. Michel Platini and Zinedine Zidane
248. Ronaldinho
249. Xabi Alonso
250. Papa Bouba Diop
251. Kaka
252. Denis Cheryshev
253. Wesley Sneijder
254. Gaizka Mendieta
255. Colombia, Argentina and Ecuador

Round 18: Forwards 2nd Round

256. Which Portuguese forward captained his side at the 2010, 2014 and 2018 World Cups?

257. Which striker won the Golden Ball Award at the 1994 World Cup?

258. Which player received the Golden Ball Award at the 2014 World Cup?

259. Can you name the forward that received the Golden Ball Award at the 1970 World Cup?

260. Which striker received the Golden Ball Award at the 1998 World Cup?

261. Who is England's all-time top goal scorer at World Cups with 10 goals?

262. Which player has scored the most goals for the Republic of Ireland at World Cups?

263. Who is the only English player to win the Best Young Player Award at a World Cup?

264. Which player won the Best Young Player Award at the 2018 World Cup?

265. Can you name the Chilean forward that scored four goals during World Cup 1998?

266. Which two forwards finished as the joint second goal scorers at the 2002 World Cup with five goals?

267. Who won the Silver Boot Award after scoring four goals at the 2018 World Cup?

268. Who started as the central forward for the Netherlands in the 2010 World Cup final?

269. Which Italian striker won the Golden Boot Award at the 1990 World Cup?

270. Can you name the player that won the Golden Ball Award at the 1974 World Cup?

Round 18 Answers

256. Cristiano Ronaldo
257. Romario
258. Lionel Messi
259. Pele
260. Ronaldo
261. Gary Lineker
262. Robbie Keane
263. Michael Owen
264. Kylian Mbappe
265. Marcelo Salas
266. Rivaldo and Miroslav Klose
267. Antoine Griezmann
268. Robin van Persie
269. Salvatore Schillaci
270. Johan Cruyff

Round 19: Penalty Shootout Trivia

271. Only one French player missed a penalty in the shootout in the 2006 final. Can you name him?

272. England finally won their first penalty shootout at a World Cup in 2018. Which nation did they beat on penalties?

273. Which player hit the last penalty over the bar in the 1994 World Cup final shootout?

274. Who scored Brazils second penalty in the 1994 World Cup final shootout? It was a great penalty that hit the post and went in.

275. Can you name the team that won two penalty shootouts at the 2018 World Cup?

276. Which Portuguese player scored the decisive last penalty to knock England out of the competition in the quarter finals of the 2006 World Cup?

277. Can you name the two English players that missed their penalties in England's 1998 penalty shootout defeat to Argentina?

278. Which team featured in the only two penalty shootouts at World Cup 2002?

279. Can you name the team that has the best record in World Cup penalty shootouts? They have played four and have a 100% win record.

280. Which team did Brazil win a penalty shootout against in the semi-finals of World Cup 1998?

281. Can you name the only English player that scored his penalty in England's 2006 quarter final defeat to Portugal?

282. Which team did Argentina win a penalty shootout against in the semi-finals of World Cup 2014?

283. Which team lost the first ever World Cup penalty shootout? This was at the semi-final stage of the 1982 World Cup.

284. Can you name the only team that won two penalty shootouts at the 1990 World Cup?

285. Which two players missed penalties for England in their semi-final shootout defeat to Germany at World Cup 1990?

Round 19 Answers

271. David Trezeguet
272. Colombia
273. Roberto Baggio
274. Romario
275. Croatia
276. Cristiano Ronaldo
277. Paul Ince and David Batty
278. Spain
279. Germany
280. Netherlands
281. Owen Hargreaves
282. Netherlands
283. France
284. Argentina
285. Stuart Pearce and Chris Waddle

Round 20: Challenging Trivia

286. Who were the first brothers to play against each other for different nations in a World Cup game?

287. Who are the two people that have won the World Cup as the captain of their nation and then later went on to win the competition as a manager?

288. Can you name the striker that won the Golden Ball Award at the 2010 World Cup?

289. Who is the only goalkeeper to win the Golden Ball Award?

290. Only one player has scored a hat-trick at two different World Cups. Can you name him?

291. Can you name the two Belgian players that have scored the most goals for their country at World Cups? Both players have scored five goals in the competition.

292. Can you name Uruguay's leading appearance maker at World Cups?

293. Who is Germany's third highest all-time goal scorer at World Cups with 11 goals in the competition?

294. Which goalkeeper received the Golden Glove Award at the 2018 World Cup?

295. Who is the only player from the Netherlands to win the Best Young Player Award at a World Cup?

296. Can you name the three German players that have won the Best Young Player Award at World Cups?

297. Which three Italian players are the top scorers at World Cups for their country? All three players have scored nine goals in the competition.

298. Can you name the two players that have scored a headed hat-trick in a World Cup game?

299. Which Argentinian player received both the Golden Ball and the Golden Boot Awards at the 1978 World Cup?

300. At the 2010 World Cup, there were four joint top goal scorers all with five goals in the competition. Can you name them?

Round 20 Answers

286. Jerome Boateng and Kevin-Prince Boateng
287. Franz Beckenbauer and Didier Deschamps
288. Diego Forlan
289. Oliver Kahn
290. Gabriel Batistuta
291. Marc Wilmots and Romelu Lukaku
292. Fernando Muslera
293. Jurgen Klinsmann
294. Thibaut Courtois
295. Marc Overmars
296. Franz Beckenbauer, Lukas Podolski and Thomas Muller
297. Paolo Rossi, Roberto Baggio and Christian Vieri
298. Tomas Skuhravy and Miroslav Klose
299. Mario Kempes
300. Thomas Muller, David Villa, Wesley Sneijder and Diego Forlan

Congratulations!

You have completed all 20 rounds of the FIFA World Cup Quiz.

There will be more quiz books coming your way soon by QuizGuy, so please keep this in mind. Please find the details of other quiz books by QuizGuy on the next page.

One last thing………

If you have enjoyed the quiz book, please write a review about this publication. This is helpful for the author and it will provide useful feedback.

Other work by QuizGuy.

ENGLISH PREMIER LEAGUE QUIZ (1992-2020)

300 FOOTBALL QUESTIONS ON PLAYER RECORDS, STATISTICS, TRANSFERS, TROPHIES & LOTS MORE TO TEST YOUR KNOWLEDGE

QuizGuy

UEFA CHAMPIONS LEAGUE QUIZ

300 QUESTIONS ON PLAYERS, TEAMS, TROPHIES & LOTS MORE TO TEST YOUR KNOWLEDGE

QuizGuy